YORK

THE SECOND CITY

JARROLD

YORK, THE SECOND CITY
Pictures Richard Tilbrook
Words John Shannon
Design Geoff Staff
Editor Helen Thompson

Designed and produced by Parke Sutton Limited, Norwich
for Jarrold Publishing, Norwich.

ISBN 0 7117 0507 0

YORK
THE SECOND CITY

Pictures Richard Tilbrook
Words John Shannon

JARROLD

YORK
THE SECOND CITY

Eboracum to the Romans, Eoforwic to the Anglo Saxons, Jorvik to the Vikings, was founded by the Romans in AD 71 — one year after Titus and his Roman armies had sacked Jerusalem, a disaster so often foretold by Christ. Let us set this city in historical perspective by remembering that there must have been Roman soldiers here whose fathers lived in the time of Christ, and as soldiers are wont to do, will have told the story to their sons — indeed some of them may have seen Christ himself. When the Spanish Armada sailed for England in 1586 the city was already some 1,500 years old; it was over 1,700 years old at the time of the Declaration of Independence of the United States of America. Such is the measure of the antiquity of York. But York's history has been made, and its buildings created, by people — people such as Roman Emperors Hadrian, Severus, Constantius and Constantine, early churchmen like Paulinus, Wilfred, Cuthbert, Alcuin and Bede; many Danish kings including one unbelievably called Eric Bloodaxe; early English kings such as Athelstan, Canute and Harold, William the Conqueror, William Rufus; and every King of England from John to Henry VIII, and every monarch of the Stuart dynasty except William and Mary and Queen Anne. In modern times names like Rowntree and Terry have made a contribution to the social and economic well being of the city's inhabitants which has secured them a well-deserved place in any history of York. Add to the list those with a more dubious claim to fame such as Guy Fawkes and Dick Turpin. It was Edmund Burke who said that a civil society is a partnership not only between those who are living but between those who are dead and those who are unborn. York is such a civil society and its history is rich evidence of that.

THE ROMANS

York sits in the middle of the mainly agricultural Vale of York, at the confluence of two rivers, the Ouse and the Foss. This it was that caused the Romans, with their military prescience, to recognise that here was a defensible site from which the whole of northern England could be governed. So it was that the Roman commander Petilius Cerialis established the new headquarters under where the Minster stands today — and the remains can still be seen. It was the forerunner of the military northern command in England which has lasted until the present time. The influence of the Romans on York cannot be overestimated — they were a race centuries before their time and they left a rich legacy which we can still see and enjoy today. Some of the streets in the historic core of the city are on the lines established by the Romans. Petergate is on the line of the Via Principalis, Stonegate on what was the Via Praetoria and Chapter House Street on the Via Decumana.

Although the Roman occupation represents only a relatively small part of York's long history it should nevertheless be set in perspective by the fact that the Romans were in England for the same period of time as has elapsed since Charles I was king. Considering the size of Roman York it is perhaps rather surprising that there is so little evidence above ground of their occupation, though what remains is of compelling interest. In the Museum Gardens is the Multangular Tower, which stands to a height of nineteen feet. The Roman structure was built on in medieval times, and the two styles of building can still be seen today. It was one of the interval towers of the Roman legionary fortress, but is the only one visible above ground. The other major Roman monument to be seen is the Roman column opposite the south door of the Minster in Deangate. It was originally one of 36 such columns which supported the great Cross Hall of the legionary fortress and was discovered a few years ago when, in a massive restoration of the Minster itself, it was found many feet below ground, lying one great drum of stone next to another, just as it had toppled over. It was given to the York Civic Trust who re-erected it not very far from where it would originally have stood, to mark the 1,900th anniversary of the city's foundation. No other monument so eloquently conveys the size of the Roman fortress, which was shaped like a playing-card, and covered an area of 50 acres. It was always known that it lay under the Minster and the excavations at the time of the restoration revealed some of its original walls which can be seen today in the museum called The Foundations beneath the Minster. The fortress was inhabited by no fewer than 6,000 soldiers.

The Roman settlement in York was one of the first examples in England of an urban development, because adjoining the military fortress was a civil town, situated south west of the River Ouse. It was important enough to be styled and given the privileges of a 'colonia' (official recognition as a town), possibly by the Emperor Severus. The large Roman garrison was, one might say, sustained by the tradesmen, camp followers and others of the town, who in their turn benefited from their attachment to a military base the size of Eboracum.

When the Romans divided Britain into two provinces, Emperor Severus designated York as the capital of Lower Britain (Britannia Inferior) and here was the home of the Imperial Court. When the Emperor Constantius I died here, his son Constantine the Great was proclaimed Emperor in York, and when he called a council of western bishops in Arles in 314, one of those present was the Bishop of York. A church in York, which still stands to this day, is dedicated to St Helen, after Constantine's mother (who was said to be the one who found the True Cross).

There are more reminders of the Romans to be found beneath the city — for instance, substantial remains of Roman sewers, and under the Roman Bath Inn in St Sampson's Square, a well preserved Roman bath house can be seen in the cellars. In fact, part of the pub has a glass floor, through which the Roman remains can be seen.

When the Romans first set up their legionary fortress in York it was during the campaigns Petilius Cerialis waged against the local tribe, the Brigantes. The legion used was the Ninth Legion, known as Hispana because it had been engaged in warfare in Spain. Sometime between 108 and 122 the legion left York, and considerable speculation abounds as to what happened to it because it disappeared without trace after AD 117, and its fate will perhaps always be a mystery. Some say it was disgraced, some say it was annihilated and some say it went from York to the continent but no evidence has ever been found. It was replaced by the Sixth Legion, which remained in the city until the end of the Roman occupation in about 400 AD. Suffice it to say that when the Romans eventually left, they left a rich legacy of history behind them and secure and lasting foundations for York.

The Emperor
Septimius Severus

THE ANGLO SAXONS

The next period in York's history, and possibly the least well documented, was occupied by the Anglo Saxons. Although little remains to be seen above ground of the Anglo Saxon period apart from the tower of St Mary Bishophill Junior and the Anglian Tower behind the city library, they made a significant contribution to the history of York, and of England. Not least of their achievements is the impressive contribution they made to the spread of Christianity, establishing many local churches. In one of them, St Mary in Castlegate (now the home of the exhibition 'The York Story') may still be seen the dedication stone of an eleventh-century church recording forever the Anglo Saxon names of Grim and Aese as two of its founders.

The Eboracum of the Romans had become the Eoforwic of the Anglo Saxons, part of eighth-century Northumbria. This was a period when some of the most significant contributions to the religious life of England were made. For here it was that Paulinus became the first Bishop of York and baptised King Edwin on Easter Day 627. Bede was to become one of the great early historians and religious figures in the country and told the story (a feature of children's history books) of Pope Gregory who, on seeing the fair haired and cherubic Anglo Saxon children said 'Non angli sed angeli' — 'these are not angles but angels'. York became the early home of Alcuin, a scholar of great distinction who was later to make a significant contribution to the court of Charlemagne. So, although these were known as the Dark Ages, there were indeed some brilliant shafts of light. But men die and history moves on. York was about to enter the period of two centuries from 866 to 1066 when, under Scandinavian and Anglo-Scandinavian domination it was to assume a new importance in the life of the nation.

THE VIKINGS

Few races are surrounded by as many myths as the Vikings — a commonly held one depicts them as having horns growing out of their helmets, though there is not the slightest evidence to support this. What we do know is that they were a warlike race who persistently attacked England, and ravaged, raped and plundered the local populations. They came to York across the seas and up the river, as it were through York's front door. Bloodthirsty they may have been, but there is now overwhelming evidence to suggest that once they had settled down they became a very civilised race of which the Jorvik Viking Centre provides profuse evidence. The Centre attracts millions of people and is one of the most visited museums in the country, the very name exciting the thousands of children who come. One of the secrets of its success is that it was created on the very site which had been excavated to reveal the Viking settlement.

Eoforwic had become the Danish Jorvik, and though little of it remains, sufficient has been discovered to demonstrate the tremendous contribution which the Vikings made to York. The archaeological excavation in Coppergate in 1980 demonstrated evocatively the full extent of the Viking settlement, and particularly the way they lived. In the Jorvik Viking Centre today can be seen the original wooden walls of the Viking homes and many of the thousands of artefacts found during the excavation, including objects from as far away as Samarkand in Asia. A potent daily reminder of Viking York can be seen in the names of nearly every street in the historic core of the city which end in the word 'gate', — Coppergate, Feasegate, Micklegate, Petergate, Spurriergate, — 'gate' or 'gata' coming from the Scandinavian word 'gata' meaning a street or way. The site of the palace of the Viking kings is still known as King's Square and on the riverside beside the appropriately named Viking Hotel there is a slipway called 'Dublin Stones' — marking the site at which they forded the river on their way across the Pennines to and from Dublin. Jorvik had become the established capital of the Danelaw — that area of England partitioned off from the south-westerly region which still remained under King Alfred's rule.

THE NORMANS

The period of Scandinavian and Anglo-Scandinavian rule was to end with the coming of William of Normandy; England prior to that time having been made up of fragmentary kingdoms which eventually came together under King Harold Godwinson. But the Vikings were not to yield up their conquests easily and a great battle was fought at Stamford Bridge some eight miles from York between Harald Hardrada of Norway and Harold of England. It was said by Winston Churchill to be one of the most decisive contests in English history. For with the dawn the River Derwent flowed with blood, the Norwegian King was dead and Harold and what remained of his army returned to York to rest. But the rest was to be short-lived, for word soon reached Harold that William of Normandy had landed in southern England. So, force-marching his battle-worn army 250 miles to the south coast, Harold met his conqueror, William of Normandy, afterwards to be crowned king in Westminster Abbey. Thus within a short period of three weeks the whole course of English history had been changed — and York's history with it. One is left to ruminate on what

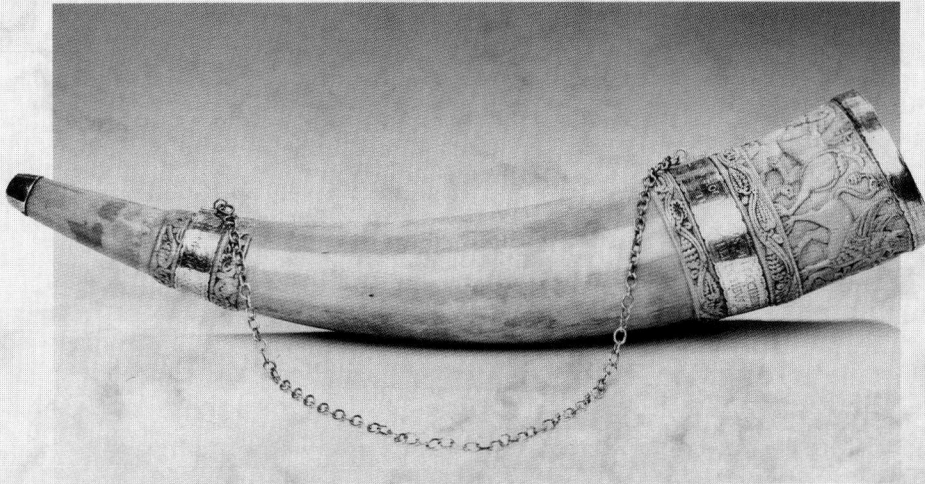

The Horn of Ulf

would have happened if Harold had lost the Battle of Stamford Bridge or indeed had not had to fight it at all. But history is full of such questions.

One of the fascinating relics of this era can be seen in the underground treasury of the Minster — the Horn of Ulf or Ulphus. It is made from ivory and probably comes from the early eleventh century. By the fourteenth century it was already in the Minster and it is said to be a horn of tenure, a token of a gift of land by Thegn Ulf, son of Thorald.

William soon dispersed his Norman knights throughout the length and breadth of England. He, like the Romans, Anglo-Saxons and Vikings before him, saw that York was a natural fortress and he quickly established his army in the city. York was not, however, to be so easily dominated — but a rising in 1068 was easily suppressed by William, who built a castle in the city, the mound of which survives to this day, and upon which stands Clifford's Tower. In 1069 a more serious rising occurred and this time William returned with great ferocity, razing the city to the ground and ravaging the countryside for miles around before he settled down to spend Christmas amidst the ruins. But it was out of those same ruins that the prosperity of York began to emerge, and we have to thank William's Domesday Book for a very accurate record of land-use in the city and its surrounding areas. The city strengthened its role as market town for a very wide area of Yorkshire, a characteristic it has preserved to this day and which was to prove its salvation. So York became the county town of the largest shire in England. The kings of the Norman period strengthened the city's defences, created a large fish-pond, and at the other end of the scale built a great cathedral, almost as big as the present day Minster. It was painted white with the outline of the stones in red and must have looked an incredible sight on a sunlit day. In time William Fitzherbert, the king's nephew, was to become Archbishop of York (an early exercise, one might say, of nepotism). When he entered the city such was the weight of the great crowd on Ouse Bridge, that it collapsed. William is said to have prayed that no-one should be drowned and none did. The 'miracle' led after his death to public clamour that he should be canonised, and he became St William in 1226 — his tomb a place of pilgrimage, and one of the finest medieval buildings in the city is named after him — St William's College.

The legacy left by the Normans is a rich one. Not only did they build a large cathedral, they also founded many of the twenty parish churches which survive to this day together with various friaries and St Mary's Abbey. This great Benedictine monastery was founded in 1088 by William II, Earl Siward of Northumbria, primarily to provide for the monks who had fled from Whitby. It was one of the great abbeys of England and, in its day, one of the wealthiest, surrounded by its own crenellated walls. The abbot was a person to be reckoned with and more than one dispute arose between him and the city. In 1132 some of the monks of the abbey church considered that their life was too soft and a party of them left the abbey and themselves founded the great Cistercian Abbey of Fountains near Ripon, perhaps the best-known abbey in England.

It was William the Conqueror who created the office of Sheriff — which derives from the words 'Shire Reeve' — and was applied to the king's representative in a county. In this connection it is interesting to note that the three Ridings of York (before the 1974 reorganisation) being counties in their own right each had a High Sheriff whereas York, at the point where the three Ridings met but not in any of them, also had a Sheriff because it was a county in its own right — the County of the City of York. However, in a fit of bureaucratic tidiness the three Ridings were swept away and York's status as a county with them. The city council petitioned the Queen to allow them to continue to have a sheriff; this was granted and there is therefore still a Sheriff of York today, who, though shorn of his legal powers still remains as a living reminder of an important figure in the city's history.

William the Conqueror, having suffered from more than one uprising by the English, imposed throughout his kingdom a curfew, (derived from the Norman French 'Couvrir feu' — to put out the fire), and until quite recently the curfew rang out every night at 8.00 pm from the tower of St Michael's, Spurriergate, which was originally a Norman church in the gift of the Conqueror.

Another Norman building of note is St Leonard's Hospice just within the entrance to the Museum Gardens. Dedicated to St Peter and believed to have been founded by King Athelstan as a hospital, it accommodated no fewer than 229 patients. Some 700 years later a new hospice in York bears the same name and carries on the same tradition of caring as its forebear.

It is said that history has a habit of repeating itself and the mass suicide of the Jews at Masada was to find its echo in York in 1190 when in a waive of anti-semitism the Jews of York, given protection by the Sheriff in Clifford's Tower, were besieged, and thinking themselves betrayed, committed mass suicide, those who did not being massacred by the mob. The Jewish community at this time was one of the largest and wealthiest in England led by Aaron of York, but was finally reduced to insignificance by the Crown's policy of taxation. Coincidence or not, the Jews have never since that day in 1190 returned to York in any significant numbers.

No history of York and its Minster is complete without reference to Archbishop Walter de Grey (1216-1255), for he it was who commenced the building of the cathedral we see today by erecting in the south transept — it must have looked huge to the inhabitants of the houses clustered around — and was effectively a challenge to those who came after the archbishop to build the rest of the great church to the same scale. His tomb is, fittingly, in the south transept. In 1968 it became necessary to dismantle the superstructure of the tomb in order to restore it and when the builders got down to ground level they found the actual coffin lid, with the archbishop's effigy painted upon it in full colour. In the presence of various church dignitaries and architectural historians, the tomb was opened and there lay what still remained of the archbishop with his pastoral staff, silver parcle-gilt chalice and paten and his ring which was adorned with a sapphire, rubies and emeralds. It was even possible to discern the pattern on the pillow upon which his head had rested, and in the skilful hands of conservationists it was possible to accurately re-create the pattern. This now appears, done by modern broderers, in the kneelers and on the altar frontal next to the tomb. The original painting, carefully restored, can now be seen in the treasury of the Minster along with the chalice paten and ring. If anyone should question the propriety of opening a tomb like this and removing the contents the answer in this case surely lies in the profound belief that the archbishop would be delighted to think that seven centuries later his life and work achieved a new reality — his Christian message echoing down the years.

THE MEDIEVALISTS

So York moved into the thirteenth and fourteenth centuries. The great Norman cathedral built by Archbishop Thomas of Bayeux in 1089 was replaced by the beginnings of the present Minster started by Archbishop de Grey, a work which was to go on for the next 250 years until the completion of the north west tower in 1472. But in the interim under the three Edwards York was to find itself the second capital of England and a base from which those kings could conduct the bitter wars against the Scots.

Perhaps even more than the Minster, the city walls are the feature which most attracts the attention of the visitor. For whereas other cities have cathedrals, none have walls like York. Nearly three miles in length, they form an almost complete circuit of the medieval city and can be walked along for the whole of their length. Built of magnesian limestone from Tadcaster they are built on top of a great earth rampart, and in this respect are unlike any others in Britain. Their origins lie in the Roman Walls of the legionary fortress which were later covered by earth during the Viking times, when they would have been topped by a wooden palisade. The stone walls which can be seen today were built in medieval times on top of those earlier ramparts. The replacement in stone of the earlier defences commenced in the middle of the thirteenth century, in the early years of Henry III's reign, and continued for the next 100 years. They are the most complete in England and in them can be seen work of the Roman, Saxon and medieval periods and in this they are unique. York also retains all four of its original 'bars', or gateways. During the middle of the nineteenth century, falling into disrepair, they were threatened with destruction by successive city councils

The city walls, circa 1882

but despite the loss of three of the barbicans, the walls themselves survived and today provide a fascinating way of viewing the medieval city within from roof level.

The city had by now become a centre for the great instruments of state; the Exchequer, Chancery and Royal Law Courts were set up by Edward I and remained in York for some seven years. For a time it was the home of Parliament and the Royal Mint. It all conjures up the picture of a castellated city, the bells of the Minster and its parish churches ringing out in the sunshine over a city of charming medieval timbered buildings, morris dancers in the streets and ladies in conical hats leaning out of upstairs windows. But the reality was far removed from such an idealistic picture. When, in 1332 Edward III established his parliament in York he complained to the mayor about the 'abominable smell abounding in the city more than in any other city in the realm from dung and manure'. Six centuries later Viscount Esher in his report on York described it as having been 'A city of exquisite architecture rising out of a midden'.

York was now reaching the zenith of its power, a great military centre, a market town, and the home of many guilds. Perhaps the best known of the guildhalls is the one that lies immediately behind the Mansion House. Begun in 1449 it was originally built by the guilds of St Christopher and St George. Although it was destroyed in the air raid on the city in 1942, it was rebuilt in facsimile. Each of the pillars is a single oak donated by the county families of Yorkshire. The building figures prominently in the history of the city and in 1583 was the scene of a Court of Enquiry set up by Elizabeth I to investigate charges against Mary, Queen of Scots. The first secular plays to be held in the city were held in the Guildhall at the time of the Armada. In 1643 the ammunition which Queen Henrietta Maria had brought from Holland to assist the loyalist cause was stored in the Guildhall and used in the defence of the city during the siege of the following year. It was in the Guildhall that five years later, in 1648, £200,000 was paid to the Scottish army on behalf of the English parliament, and it is recorded that it took the Scots twelve days to count it, a fact which may surprise no one. In 1688 it was the scene of the Declaration of Loyalty to William of Orange. At one time the assizes were held here, the grand court at one end and the court of Nisi Prius at the other. York enjoyed a prosperity far above that of most English cities and became with Norwich, Bristol and London one of the largest cities of the kingdom (even so, at its zenith, the population rarely exceeded 15,000 people). It became a flourishing port, hard though this might be to believe today, but the river which the Vikings had seen as the highway to the heart of York was also the highway along which a great trade would develop with all the northern ports of Europe, chiefly through the influence of guilds like the Merchant Adventurers' Company, whose Hall can still be seen intact in York today.

The Merchant Adventurers' Hall is a superb medieval monument in a remarkable state of preservation. The Merchant Adventurers (the Company still exists today) traded with all the ports of northern Europe and exercised tremendous power over trade in the city, with great powers of patronage. The Hall itself was built between 1357 and 1361 from local oak trees from the Vale of York. It has an undercroft and a chapel built or rebuilt in 1411. For anyone interested in the medieval period of York's history a visit to the Hall is essential. The walls like the walls of the city, were built from Tadcaster stone. Richard II (1377 — 1399) came to York on at least nine occasions and clearly it became his favourite city. Several charters were granted by him, one of which gave York county status, and the mayor, who was to become known as the Lord Mayor, was given two Sheriffs as supporters. The Lord Mayor of York is today second only to the Lord Mayor of London. Until modern times, when the honour was extended to the capital cities of the United Kingdom, only the Lord Mayors of York and London were entitled to the prefix 'The Right Honourable'. York also retains to this day its position as the second city in England.

The city had by now extended beyond the medieval walls and despite the bubonic plague, managed to survive. The late fourteenth century saw the highlight of York's prosperity in the Middle Ages, but such prosperity was to be brief because by 1450 the city had begun to decline, disease was rampant, poverty was rife and the city was overcrowded by those newcomers who had looked on it as a source of wealth and prosperity. Even so, it was the second richest city in England with a big export trade in wool. But the decline continued; the city's importance as a port diminished as the river silted up and as Hull took over this role, but paradoxically enough the city was about to enter upon its greatest period of building. The completion of the Minster in 1472 (by now the largest cathedral north of the Alps) and the building of two great guildhalls, St Mary's Benedictine Abbey and no fewer than 45 parish churches was to give York an architectural legacy which has survived to this day, although the number of churches has diminished to one half of their original number. Of these, two are most worthy of mention: All Saints, North Street with some of the finest parish church stained glass in England, and Holy Trinity, Goodramgate with its box pews and fifteenth-century East Window (a rare date in York glass) and its marvellous atmosphere. The streets were beginning to be paved, better drainage systems introduced and gutters and fall pipes introduced. Nevertheless York, from being the wealthiest provincial city under Richard II, became only fourteenth under Henry VIII and the Wars of the Roses did nothing to stem the tide of recession. When one recalls the fierce rivalry between York and Lancaster which continues in a more civilised manner to this day, it is hard to believe that the City of York itself became for a time a Lancastrian stronghold. When the Duke of York was killed at Wakefield his head was set up on Micklegate Bar, an event which is recalled in Shakespeare's Henry VI when Queen Margaret says 'Off with his head and set it on York's gates so York may overlook the town of York'. But the tide was soon to turn and when the Duke's son became Edward VI, having won the Battle of Towton on Palm Sunday, 1461 (one of the bloodiest battles of the Wars of the Roses), York again assumed its Yorkshire pride and it was Lancastrian heads which took the place of the Yorkists on Micklegate Bar. One of the most maligned characters in English history, Richard, Duke of Gloucester, was to become king as Richard III in 1483. He became a great friend of York and did all he could to revive its prosperity. So great was his contribution that on hearing of his death at Bosworth the City Council recorded in their minutes that 'King Richard, late mercifully reigning upon us was piteously slain and murdered to the great heaviness of this city'.

It was about this time that St William's College was built under Letters Patent granted to Warwick the Kingmaker by Edward IV to house some 24 of the chantry priests of the Minster, whose unbecoming conduct in the streets of York at night had caused no little consternation. Situated near the East End of the Minster it is in a remarkable state of preservation. During the Civil War Charles I had his printing presses here.

Lying just behind St William's College is the Treasurer's House. A site of various buildings since Roman times (the base of a Roman column can still be seen in a cellar passage near Chapter House Street), it is so called because it was for many years the home of the Treasurers of York Minster, an office established by Thomas of Bayeux whom William the Conqueror had appointed as Archbishop. Up to 1162 the first four Treasurers to be appointed appear to have lived in York. There is probably no other house in York which contains architectural features spanning as many centuries — from the twelfth to the nineteenth. Much of the twelfth-century masonry can be seen in the lower parts of the house. The main south-west elevation is early seventeenth century. The house was surrendered to the Crown in 1547 by the last Treasurer (giving the unanswerable reason that there was no treasure left). From the king the house passed to the Lord Protector, Somerset, and eventually in the time of Cromwell to Lord Fairfax. Over the years the house has been renovated several times but the banqueting hall is one of the original features which survives. In July 1746 the Duke of Cumberland, the 'bloody butcher of Culloden' on his way back to London from his campaign against the Scottish Jacobites, was entertained here by the Archbishop of York and was given the freedom of the city. After many vicissitudes the house was given to the National Trust in 1930.

York's fortunes continued to decline, revived only for a short time in the reign of Henry VII who in 1503 created the King's Council in the North housed in the Kings Manor, bringing administration and justice for the northerners. It was to be strengthened by Henry VIII and gave a new if short lived prosperity to the city. It brought to the city a good deal of legal business and heard thousands of cases a year. Its establishment also brought in its train officers of the court, clerks, lawyers and others concerned with the administration of justice, bringing with it a great deal of trade.

St Mary's Abbey was (along with other religious foundations) suppressed by Henry VII in 1589, their treasures plundered and their books dispersed. The ruined buildings became quarries from which many other buildings in York were built. A further example of the 'recycling' of materials is to be found in many of the timber framed buildings in the city (a considerable number of which still exist today behind Georgian and Victorian facades) which were built from ships' timbers, no doubt being taken from ships rotting on the quayside in the now disused port of York. A ship's figurehead affixed incongruously to a medieval house in Stonegate no doubt came from the same source.

York was to experience the traumas of religious change and intolerance at the time of the Reformation. Robert Aske, who led the Pilgrimage of Grace, was to end up by hanging alive in chains from Clifford's Tower, and many of the parish churches were shorn of their catholic furnishings. But the unique collection of stained glass of the Minster and parish churches of the city somehow survived.

The slow decline continued throughout the reign of Queen Elizabeth when religious intolerance found its height in York in the death of St Margaret Clitheroe, found guilty of harbouring priests, and sentenced to death by pressing. The house in the Shambles in York where she is said to have lived was restored in modern times and made into a shrine. Unfortunately she is in fact now thought to have lived on the other side of the street.

The seventeenth century saw a temporary improvement in the city's prosperity punctuated by events such as the Gunpowder Plot with whom the name of Guy Fawkes has been linked ever since. He had been a pupil at St Peter's School in York, one of the oldest in Britain which survives to this day. You won't be surprised to hear that they don't have a bonfire there on Guy Fawkes night. Guy Fawkes was baptised in the church of St Michael le Belfrey in the shadow of the Minster and a nearby hotel sign claims that it was the

Detail from a seventeenth-century depiction of the Gunpowder plot, showing Guy Fawkes

Guido Fawkes

birth place of Guy Fawkes. However, we know from evidence in the Minster Library that in fact his parents lived some way away in Stonegate where there is a plaque recording the fact that his parents lived nearby.

It will be noted that the plaque is so worded as not to destroy the hotel's claim to fame. After all, Mrs Fawkes might have slipped out for a shandy . . .

The seventeenth century also saw a lively contribution by York to English history. For mid-century was the time of the Civil War when Charles I and his creed of the Divine Right of Kings found themselves arrayed against the power of Parliament. York had always been a loyalist city — the King's Arms may be seen over the entrance to the King's Manor — and its walls, built some two centuries earlier, were to play a role in its defence for the last time. The great siege of York by the Parliamentarians proved to be one of the most significant events in York's history. Indeed the king (who had dined in York with his court in happier days) saw it as one of the lynchpins in his fight. 'If York be lost' (he wrote to Prince Rupert in 1644) 'I shall esteem my crown little less'. But following the Battle of Marston Moor in 1644 the city surrendered. The commander of the Parliamentarian forces was Ferdinando, Lord Fairfax, a local landowner, who had great affection for the city. When he accepted its surrender he ordered 'that neither churches nor other buildings shall be defaced' and there is not the slightest doubt that present day York owes its survival together with its huge collection of stained glass to that magnanimous gesture by Lord Fairfax in the moment of victory. But the decline of York was to continue, despite a temporary reprieve in the seventeenth century. The city had begun, as it were to sink into its own morass, a 'dank demesne' as it had been described by Egil, the Icelander, in 948, and as the waters had preserved the Viking remains so the fabric of the city was also to be preserved. By now it had become something of a backwater in national terms and over the next century and a half it was only its traditional role of market town that saved it from the extinction which had over-whelmed many a medieval community which had lost its purpose. The people of the Vale of York, whilst not oblivious to its great role in English history, saw it primarily as a place where they could sell their wares and produce. This indeed was a late seventeenth-century 'kiss of life'. Thus the wheel of history slowly began to restore to York the importance and greatness which it had once known.

THE GEORGIANS

In the early Georgian period the nobility of the county, many of whom had descended from William the Conqueror's knights, began to see that York could be an alternative centre for their recreation, for London was a hazardous four days' journey by coach. They saw the city as a centre where they could meet to dance, play cards or go to the races (for York had been one of the earliest centres in England for the Sport of Kings), a place where they could disport themselves, flirt, and for a macabre entertainment watch poor wretches being sentenced to deportation for life at the city's Assize Courts. The city entered into a new and elegant architectural era, perhaps the best example of which lies in the Assembly Rooms, built by public subscription to a design by the Earl of Burlington in 1730 and recognised today as one of the earliest neo-classical buildings in Europe. It was designed to cater for the social activities of the county families of Yorkshire and for 'all public diversions such as assemblies, concerts of music, etc'. The main room is in the style of an Egyptian Hall. It is unquestionably the finest building of its kind and period in England (not forgetting the Assembly Rooms of Bath). The Rooms were beautifully restored by the York City Council in 1951. Added to this was the building of the great town houses of the Georgian nobility with those in Micklegate and Bootham being foremost, although without doubt the finest Georgian town house to survive in York is Fairfax House in Castlegate, recently restored by York Civic Trust to its former unique splendour. The house was built by

Charles, Ninth Viscount Fairfax

Viscount Fairfax of Emley in 1762 as, it is thought, a dowry for his surviving daughter Anne. The Viscount had had four sons and three daughters. All four sons died of smallpox and two of his daughters died, leaving Anne who was, perhaps understandably, neurotic. Fairfax employed the very finest craftsmen of the age and poured all his money into the house. A letter exists in which he wrote to his bankers in London 'My daughter's house in York which has drained me of all my moneys'. Alas, his daughter was to die unmarried and the house passed through many hands until eventually becoming a ballroom and adjunct to a cinema built alongside. It had reached a derelict state when the York Civic Trust acquired it. But despite all the maltreatment its superb plaster ceilings and carved woodwork had survived almost intact. It is a fitting background for the superb collection of Georgian furniture it houses. The collection was built up by Noel Terry, and is said to be one of the finest collections of its kind.

Another fine house in York is the Mansion House. It was built in 1725-32 as a home for the Lord Mayor and surprisingly the Minutes of the City Council at that time contain no reference to the architect, although it may have been the artist William Etty. It is interesting to reflect that London's Mansion House was not started until seven years after York's was built. The house sits very happily on one side of St Helen's Square in the city centre. It contains one of the best collections of civic plate in the country including a fascinating Georgian chamber pot in solid silver and a gold cup dating from 1673. It also houses the civic regalia, the Lord Mayor's chain having been given to the city in 1612, whilst the chain of the Lady Mayoress dates from 1670.

THE RAILWAY AGE

George Hudson, the 'Railway King'

So the city was entering a new phase of life, and it was to see yet another resurgence with the coming of the railways in the early part of the nineteenth century, largely due to the efforts of George Hudson, twice Lord Mayor of York, who was to become known as the Railway King and who had sworn 'to mak all t'railways come to York'. What Hudson realised was what the Romans had seen so many centuries earlier — that York was ideally placed as a centre of communications with the rest of the United Kingdom. So began York's role as a great railway centre, which it enjoys to this day. And how fitting it is that the railway station in York is one of the great Victorian buildings of England, finished in 1877 when it was said to be the largest station in the world. The distinguished architectural historian Patrick Nuttgens aptly described it as 'York's Propylaeum'. The railway industry, once established, was to become one of York's main sources of prosperity, but there was another which vied with it in importance and that was the chocolate industry.

CHOCOLATE AND CHARITY

Rowntree's Chocolate advertisement, 1922

The first Joseph Rowntree had come to York from Scarborough in 1822, setting up a small grocer's shop in a street called Pavement. Education was his primary interest and the foundation of The Mount and Bootham Schools owes much to him. He was succeeded by his son, also called Joseph. Ardent members of the Society of Friends, each night after the shop had closed, Joseph Rowntree and his wife brought back the boys and girls who had worked with them during the long day, and in a small room behind the shop taught them and their parents to read and to write. The shop workers learned about such far away places as India and the West Indies, which had produced the tea and sugar they sold in the shop. The Rowntrees gave new horizons to people whose only horizon was the outhouse of the next door slum. In that little room behind the shop they gave birth to the idea of adult education. As the business grew and prospered and eventually became one of the biggest chocolate factories in Europe so their ideals went with them: of employer/employee relationships, of conval-escent homes, a theatre, a library and pensions for the workers. They gave to those workers the real meaning of human dignity in an England where it had hitherto sadly been lost. Nor was that the only contribution of the Rowntree family to the welfare of York. Joseph gave one half of his wealth to the establishment of three trusts — one social, charitable and religious, one a purely social trust and the third a village trust concerned with housing and in particular with a model garden village at New Earswick, just outside York. Joseph's son Seebohm was, in his turn, to make a major contribution to the social welfare not only of York but of England in his classic work Poverty, a Study of Town Life. *It was in its way to be a progenitor of the modern welfare state. So the Rowntrees and Terrys, whose confectionery firm was established even earlier in 1767, made a unique con-tribution to the prosperity of York which survives to this day, giving, with the railways, a firm economic base to the city which it has never since lost.*

Noel Terry

Joseph Rowntree

THE 20TH CENTURY RENAISSANCE

And so we come to the twentieth century and to the second World War, up to which time the medieval city, built on Roman and Viking foundations, had survived virtually intact. It had been greatly helped in this by the fact that the discovery of coal in the west of the county had caused the Industrial Revolution to be con-centrated in that part of the region leaving the city of York virtually untouched, basically still a market town, as it had been for centuries. The coming of the second World War posed new problems for York and none more so than in the great air raid of April 1942 when in a night of terror 74 people were killed, the station hit and the Guildhall and St Martin's Church burned out. But miraculously, despite a bright moon-lit night when the Minster stood out like a great white cliff, the dawn came with the historic core of the city still virtually intact. Had the bombs that night taken the Minster and York's historic streets it would not be the same city that it is today. In the event it emerged from six years of war unkempt, unpainted and largely unscathed, but not unloved. Indeed any study of the history of York reveals that in every century there has always been a handful of people — and it has never needed more than a handful — who cared deeply for the city and sought its preservation. As far back as 1596, when a suggestion was made that Clifford's Tower be demolished, a petition from the City Council to the Lord Chancellor described it 'an exceeding orna-ment to the city' and that they would have 'no other building for showe of this cittye sarve but of onlye the Minster and church steeples if the said towre shall be pulled down'.

It was in 1946 that the York Civic Trust was founded by four York citizens, J B Morrell, Noel Terry, Oliver Sheldon and Dean Eric Milner-White, pledged to preserve the city and its antiquities for future generations to enjoy. Its terms of reference were drawn widely enough to cover not just the physical aspects of the city but its cultural life in the widest sense — covering the fields of design, craftsmanship and educa-tion. In a day and age and in a climate when conservation was largely unknown, these four men saw with great vision that it would be in the years immediately following the war that there would be a spirit of renewal abroad, a desire to sweep away the old and build anew, and it was the Civic Trust which was largely responsible for preventing this from happening. But in the 1960s there swept across England a wave of redevelopment with get-rich-quick entrepreneurs promising local authorities new city centres, dangling before them the bait of modernisation and increased rateable values. It was during this period that many of England's historic cities suffered cruelly, their historic centres torn out to be replaced by high-rise and characterless buildings of glass and concrete. The Guardian headline — 'The sack of Worcester' is

Extract from a petition against the demolition of Clifford's Tower (1596)

still remembered. Those same developers came to York but never succeeded, largely due to two factors. First an inbred inertia in the York character which resists all form of sudden change and secondly an annual change in the political balance on the City Council which thereby conspired to frustrate any forward planning.

The 1960s had taken their toll of England's historic towns to such an extent that it prompted the government of the day to select four cities to be the subject of detailed studies in order to see how historic cities could survive in the twentieth century, enjoying prosperity whilst retaining their historic character, and it was largely due to the efforts of the York Civic Trust that York was one of the four cities to be chosen, the others being Chester, Chichester and Bath. The consultant appointed for York was Viscount Esher whose 1968 report, York: a Study in Conservation, was to become a watershed in the city's long history. It is true to say that it resulted in York becoming one of the best preserved cities in England, commercially prosperous, yet retaining its unique character, having no fewer than 1,500 buildings listed as of architectural or historic importance and a more complete cycle of all ages of English architecture than any other city in Britain. One consequence of the Esher Report was that millions of pounds of government money was ploughed into York either directly or indirectly in the cause of conservation. Six years earlier the University of York, of which the York Civic Trust (through its Academic Development Committee) was the progenitor, had been established — the culmination of many years of endeavour and giving York a place in the academic life of the nation which had somewhat surprisingly escaped it over the centuries.

So York has taken its place as one of the foremost historic cities of Europe, the cultural capital of the north of England and still a bustling market town. Because of all these attributes it has become one of the most visited cities in England and the trade of tourism has added a new dimension to the city's prosperity. Most importantly it has succeeded in this without losing any of its integrity. There is no room in York for the 'Queen Elizabeth slept here' type of spurious history. If you were to ask any of its many visitors why they had come they might find it difficult to put it into words, but I suspect they come because here they can walk in streets where the Romans walked, they can see where and how the Vikings lived and William the Conqueror stayed, they can hear the echo of King Charles and his cavaliers, study the beginnings of the railways, savour the elegance of the Georgian era, and feel themselves part of the great procession of history, and, not least important, they can, almost subconsciously, savour the joy of walking in a city which has kept its human scale perhaps better than any other city in England.

Successive tides of English history have ebbed and flowed against the walls of York. For those with eyes to see the tidemarks are plainly visible.

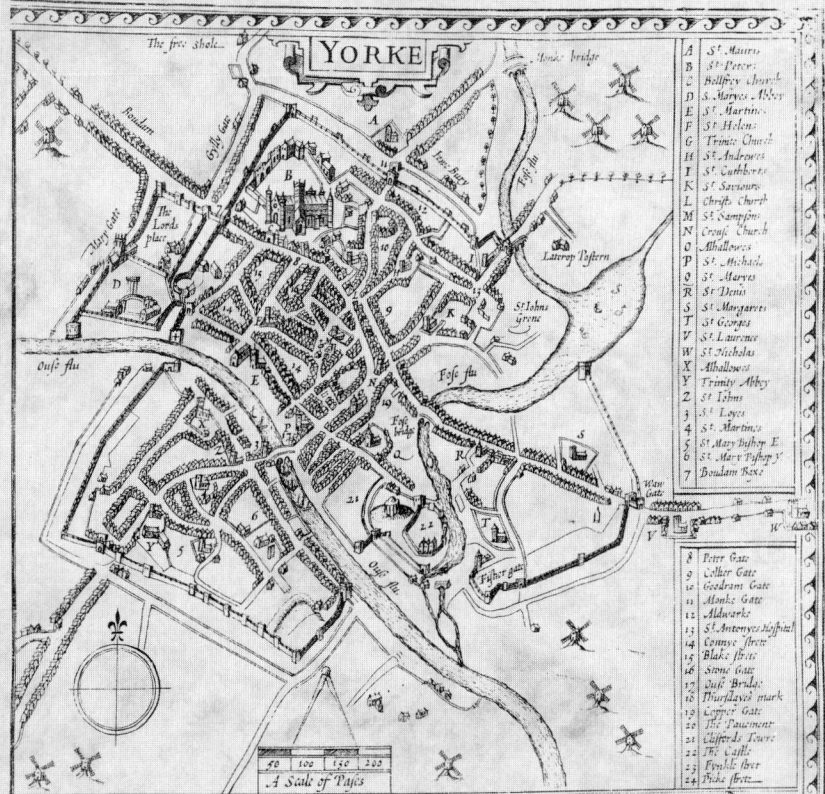

A map of York by
John Speed, 1610

The rivers of York — the Ouse and the Foss — have played a major part in its history. It was the confluence of the two rivers which the Romans saw as a natural defensive position and led to the foundation of Eboracum in 71 AD. The Ouse was a highway into the heart of the city and was so used by the Viking invaders. In medieval times York became a flourishing port. Today, little of that remains, but the river has come into its own again for sport and recreation.

THE RIVERS

Lendal Bridge, built in 1863 to replace the ferry which had operated since the middle ages (*far left*) with (*top, left*) members of the rowing club and (*bottom, left*) King's Staith.

Foss Bridge, built in 1811-12, (*right*), and Lendal Bridge and the fifteenth-century Guildhall (*below*) which still has a long vaulted passage leading down to the river.

King's Staith (*left*), once a part of the medieval port of York. Foss Bridge (*below*); and (*right*) Lendal Bridge with the Guildhall in the distance.

South Esplanade (*top, far left*) from Ouse Bridge, and (*top, left*) from one of the pleasure boats on the river, looking towards Ouse Bridge.

Lendal Bridge with the City Arms (*left*).

Ouse Bridge, which, like many medieval bridges, originally had shops and houses built on it. The weight of the buildings caused the collapse of the bridge in 1565. The present bridge was built in 1810 (*above*). Lendal Bridge with the arms of the diocese of York (*right*).

Pleasure boats on the Ouse (*left*); North Esplanade (*below, left*), and the Guildhall and St Martin's Church tower (*below*).

South Esplanade (*right*), and (*below*) the Guildhall and pleasure boats.

The streets of York are lined with numerous beautiful and historic shops, restaurants and pubs, many of which have been there for centuries. Many of the pubs, for instance, started life as coaching inns, and still retain their original layout round a courtyard. Pictured (*right*) is the Red Lion Inn, Merchantgate.

The Black Swan, Peasholme Green (*top, left*); the York Arms in Petergate (*bottom, left*); the Hansom Cab (*above*); and (*below*) Taylor's Tea Rooms, Stonegate.

The Grapes (*above*); the Golden Fleece (*below*); one of the many fine shops in Stonegate (*top, right*); and Thomas's Pub, Museum Street (*bottom, right*).

One of Stonegate's attractive windows (*right*); a butcher's shop in Petergate (*below*); a tea shop, Stonegate (*bottom, left*); a Stonegate shop (*middle, right*); and the Spread Eagle, Walmgate (*bottom, right*).

The King's Arms, King's Staith (*far right*).

The defences of York are, uniquely, almost complete, the city walls being the feature which most attracts the visitors. Nearly three miles in length, they form an almost complete circuit of the medieval city and can be walked along for the whole of their length. They are built of magnesian limestone on earlier ramparts and date from the thirteenth/fourteenth centuries. York also retains its four original bars, or gateways. Pictured (*right*) is the twelfth-century Clifford's Tower, built on a motte constructed by William the Conqueror.

Monk Bar (*left*) is the city's tallest gate. Like the other Bars, the rooms above it have had a variety of uses. In the fifteenth century, they were let at a rent of four shillings, and in the sixteenth century were used as a prison. A walk on the walls (*below*). Walmgate Bar (*top, right*); Monk Bar from the walls (*below, right*); and Micklegate Bar (*far right*). The rooms above Micklegate Bar commanded the highest rent of all the Bars — thirteen shillings and fourpence. When Richard, Duke of York, was executed in 1460, his head was displayed above the Bar.

The Water Tower, built in 1318, part of the defences of St Mary's Abbey (*above*); the Minster from the walls (*right*); the Roman Multangular Tower (*below*), built in the fourth-century strengthening of Eboracum's defences. Clifford's Tower (*left*), built in the thirteenth century, to replace an earlier wooden castle.

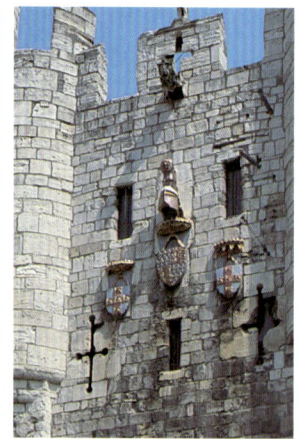

Bootham Bar from Petergate (*left*), and (*above*) looking through the Bar. Bootham Bar is on the site of the Roman Porta Principalis, one of the gates of the legionary fortress. Bootham Bar lost its barbican, along with Monk Bar and Micklegate Bar, in the nineteenth century. Micklegate Bar (*above, right*); the Walk near Monk Bar (*right*); and St Mary's Tower (*below*), scene of the failure of a Royalist attack on the Parliamentarians in 1644.

The city walls near Bootham Bar (*above*); Monk Bar from inside (*below*); the Minster from the walls (*right*).

The wall from Grey's court (*top*) and the
Multangular Tower (*left*). North Street Postern
(*below*) where the wall breaks for the river. A chain
stretched across the river from here to Lendal Tower
continued the defences. The Minster from the city
walls (*right*).

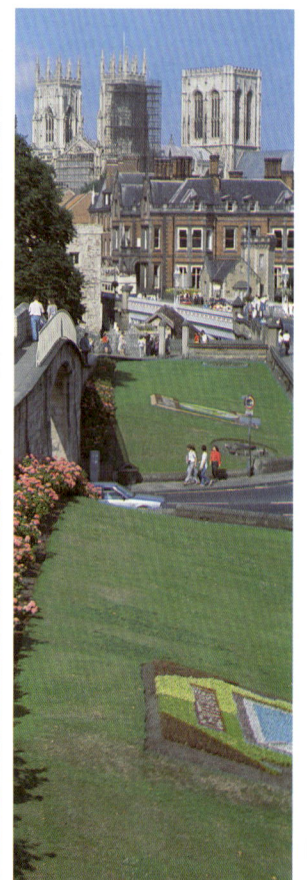

Clifford's Tower (*right*), and (*below*) Walmgate Bar, the only gate to retain its barbican. The rooms above the Bar were lived in until as recently as 1959.

York has some 1,000 listed buildings — Norman, medieval, Georgian, Victorian and modern. It has a more complete cycle of English architecture than any other English city, and most of the buildings are in a remarkable state of preservation, including some twenty medieval churches, many public houses, and the remains of a fine Benedictine Abbey. On the right is the well preserved fourteenth-century hall of the Merchant Adventurers' Company of York.

The Yorkshire Insurance building in St Helen's Square (*left*); the Treasurer's House (*below*), an amalgam of seventeenth and eighteenth-century building, now owned by the National Trust. The Railway Station (*bottom*), and (*below, left*) the City Art Gallery in Exhibition Square.

The National Railway Museum — (*below*) a sectioned locomotive, showing its workings, and (*bottom*) Queen Adelaide's Coach, built for the widow of King William IV.

The Theatre Royal (*right*).

St William's College (*left*) its frontage largely unaltered since it was built in 1460; Chapter House Street (*below*); and the Mansion House (*bottom*), home of the City of York regalia.

The Red House, Duncombe Place (*below*); Fairfax House, Castlegate, built by Viscount Fairfax for his daughter (*bottom*); and St William's College (*right*).

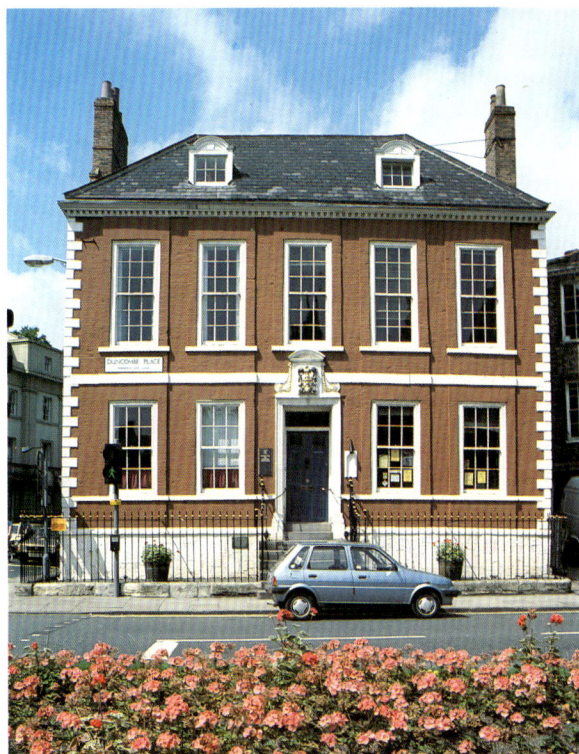

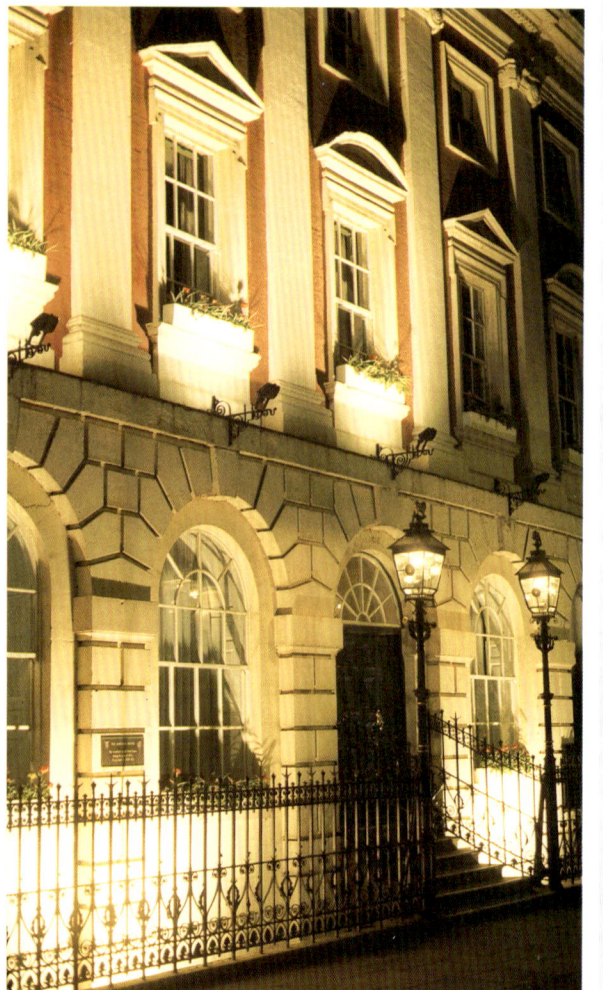

A Coney Street shop (*top, far left*), and an unusual example of Victorian tiling in Stonegate (*top, left*). Sir Thomas Herbert's House (*bottom, far left*) was built in 1616 for an old York merchant family. Sir Thomas Herbert was a Parliamentarian who converted to Charles I's Royalist cause. The Mansion House in St Helen's Square (*bottom, left*).

St William's College and its tranquil courtyard (*right*), and (*below*). The College was built to house the Minster's Chantry Priests. When Charles I moved his Court to York, he set up his printing presses in the college.

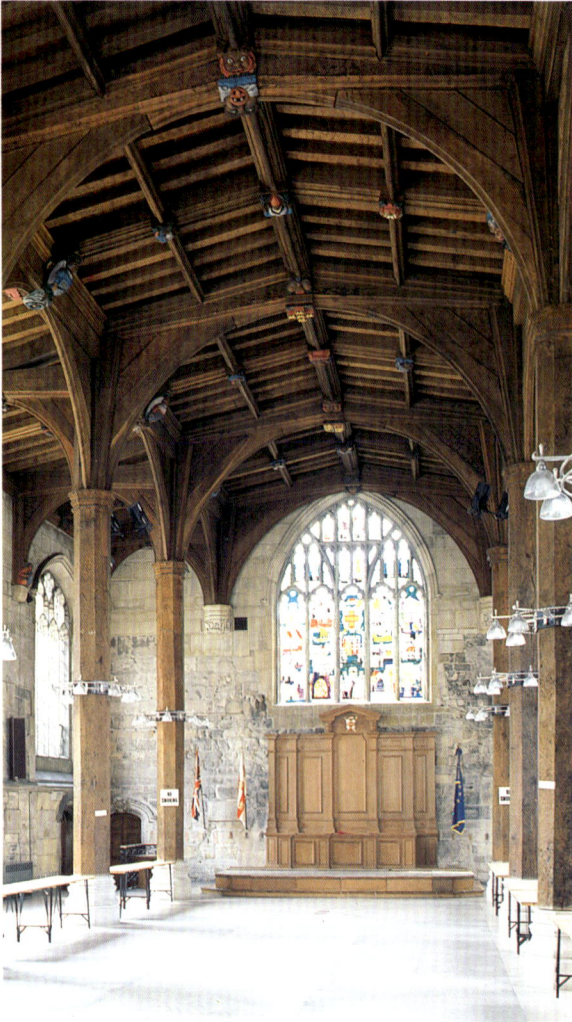

The Guildhall (*top, far left*), and Committee Room (*left*). The Guildhall was destroyed in the German air raid of 1942. It was rebuilt in facsimile. Each of the pillars in the main hall is a single oak donated by the county families of Yorkshire. The Bar Convent Museum (*bottom, left*), in the house which was given in 1686 to the nuns of the Institute of the Blessed Virgin for a school and convent; and Castle Museum (*bottom, far left*), opened in 1938, and famous for its reconstructions of streets and houses. The Merchant Adventurers' Hall (*right*) was built for the guild of Merchant Adventurers in the fourteenth century. Fairfax House, Castlegate: the staircase (*below*), the kitchen (*above, right*), and the saloon (*below, right*).

York racecourse (*left*) has provided entertainment in York since the early days of George II's reign. It stands on Knavesmire, common pasture land, on which stood the old city gallows. Micklegate House (*middle, left*). Our Lady's Row, Goodramgate (*below*) dates from the fourteenth century, and is said to be one of the oldest rows of houses in England. St Mary's Abbey (*bottom*) was built in the thirteenth century, and destroyed during the Dissolution of Monasteries.

The Treasurer's House (*above*) was built for the Treasurers of the Minster. A reconstruction of a Viking warehouse (*top, middle*) in the Jorvik Viking Centre; and the Bar Convent chapel (*top, right*). St William's College (*right*); and Castlegate House (*below*), built in 1759.

From earliest times York has been the principal market town of the vale of York and retains that characteristic today. The historic core of the city has kept its original character and scale, its narrow medieval streets on top of Roman ones, and most with the Viking suffix 'gate' — all thronged with people, and in season, packed with tourists. Pictured (*right*) is one of the pleasures of York — enjoying tea outside the Theatre Royal.

Pavement artists abound, in Pavement, (*left*), and (*bottom*) the return of the Vikings to King's Square. Buskers provide popular entertainment (*top, right*), and (*below, right*) in King's Square; al fresco eating (*below*) in King's Square.

Opposite page: Stonegate (*top, far right*); Exhibition Square (*bottom, right*); Coppergate Walk and the Jorvik Viking Centre (*extreme right*).

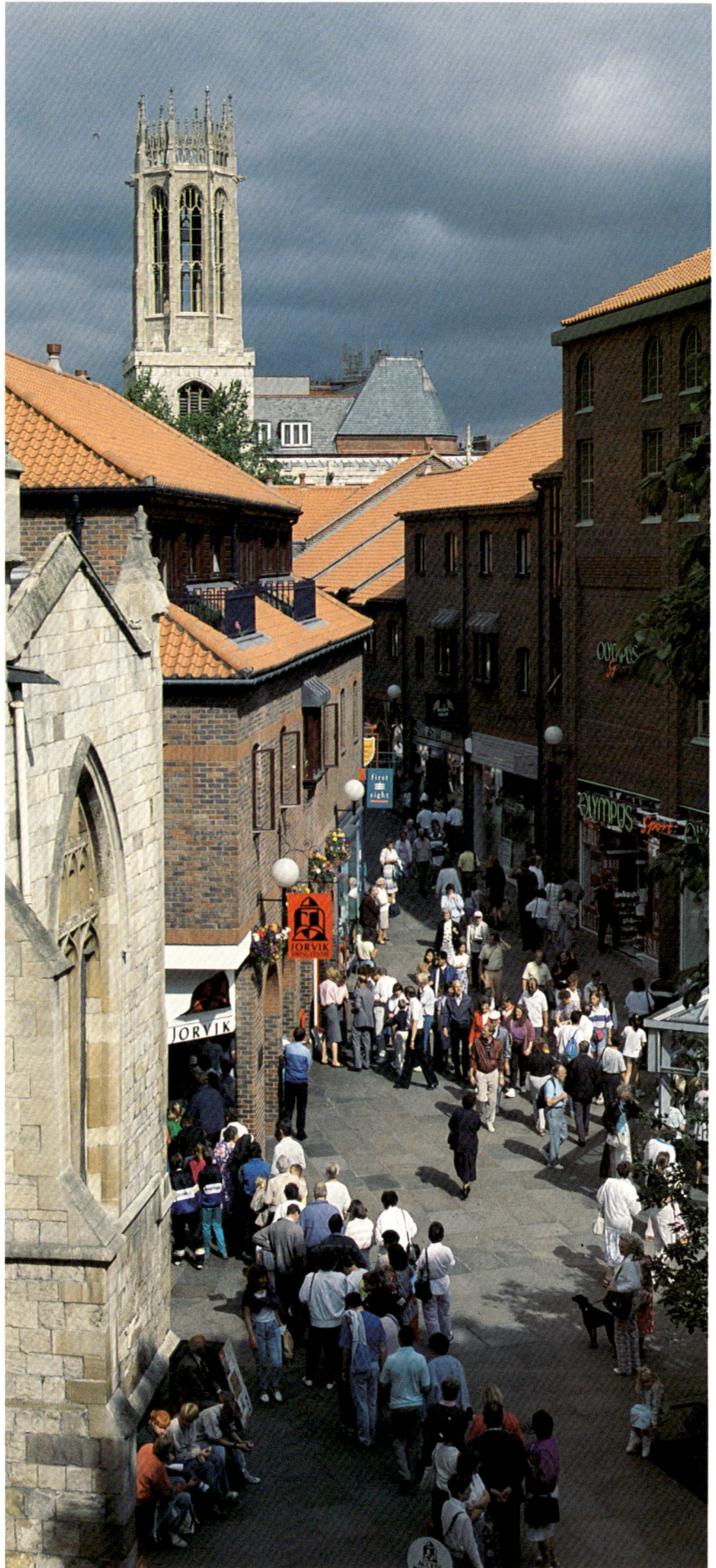

Newgate Market (*right*), and The Shambles (*below,*
left and right). The Shambles was once the street of
butchers' shops — 'Shambles' derives from the early
English word 'shamel', meaning stall or booth, upon
which the meat was displayed. The buildings, now
carefully restored, date from the fifteenth century.

The Shambles (*above*); Newgate Market (*top, right*); and Stonegate (*middle and bottom, right*). Stonegate follows the route of the Roman Via Praetoria, which led to the Headquarters of the legionary fortress, where the Minster now stands. Stonegate was the street of bookshops — York's earliest-known press was sited there in 1509.

Coppergate Walk (*above, left*); Duncombe Place (*below, left*); the station flower stall (*top*); the famous Betty's Restaurant (*above*); and (*below*) Russell's, in Stonegate.

Petergate (*left*) follows the route of the Roman Via Principalis. The Jorvik Viking Centre (*below*) was built on the site where an archaeological dig revealed valuable evidence of York's Viking past. The Shambles (*right*); and (*bottom*) Cumberland House, King's Staith. The house dates from the eighteenth century. Its front door is actually round the corner in Cumberland Street, to escape the frequent flooding of the Staith.

The Shambles (*left*); Newgate Market (*right*);
Stonegate — by day (*below*), and (*bottom*) by night.

Opposite page: St Sampson's Square (*top, left*); Punch
and Judy in St Sampson's Square (*top, middle*); the
Museum Gardens (*top, right*). Newgate Market
(*middle, left*); Parliament Street (*middle, right*); The
Shambles (*bottom, left and right*).

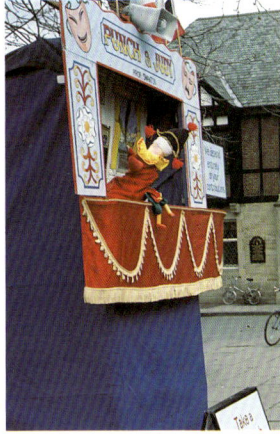

The Minster is perhaps York's best known feature. The largest cathedral north of the Alps and the biggest medieval building of any kind in England, it was built between 1220 and 1472 on the site of the earlier Norman cathedral. It has one of the finest collections of stained glass in England. The word 'minster' derives from the Latin 'monasterium', a place of Christian teaching. Pictured (*right*) is the Minster Chapter House ceiling.

The Minster from Minster Court (*left*); Chapter House Street (*right*); and (*below*) the Minster from Aldwark.

TURKS HEAD COURT

BARTLE GARTH

Three different aspects of the Minster: the West Towers (*right*); a view from the north-east (*below, right*); and from Duncombe Place (*below*).

A detail from the Choir Screen (*left*) and the Choir from the east (*below*). Evidence of earlier buildings beneath the Minster was discovered during restoration work in the 1970s. The Undercroft now houses a permanent exhibition of the history of the Minster site and of the city. The remains of Roman buildings can still be seen — part of a mural (*top left*), and a column (*below, left*).

The Choir Screen (*right and far right*) was built in
1475-1500. It contains fifteen statues of kings of
England from William the Conqueror to Henry VI
(the last is of a later date than the screen). The
South Transept (*below, right*); and (*below*) the Nave,
looking east. The Nave was begun in 1291. The roof
bosses are accurate copies of medieval ones
destroyed by fire in 1840.

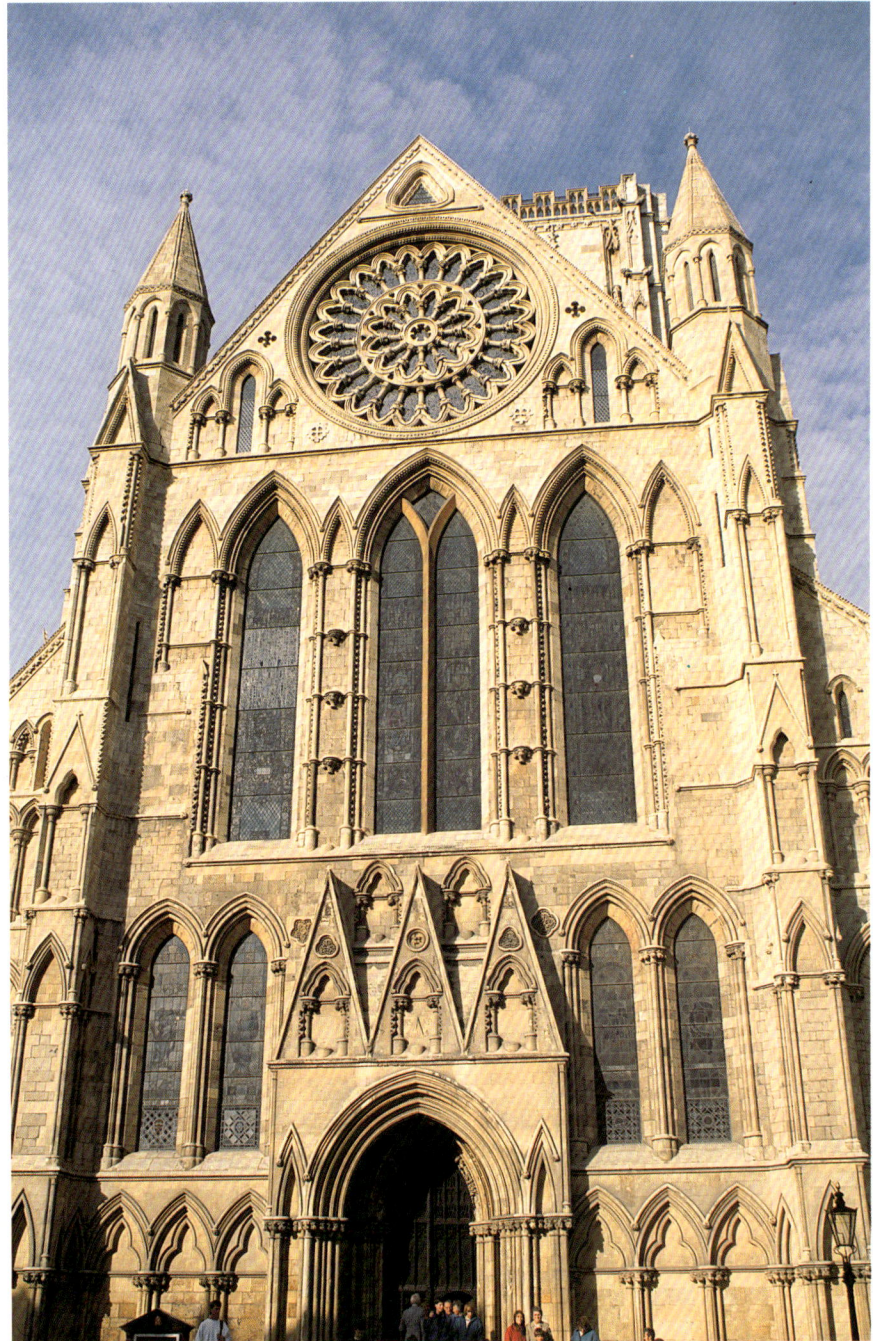

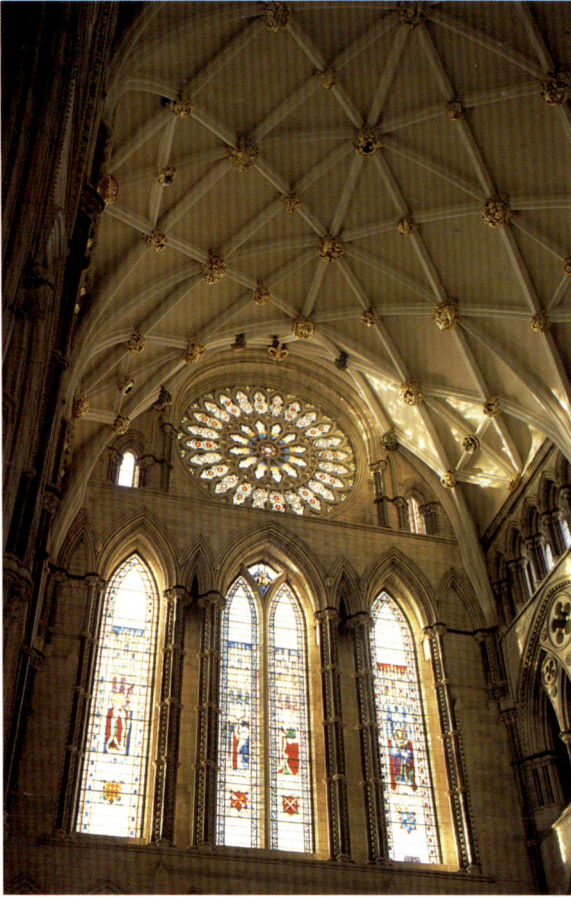

The beautiful Rose Window (*above*) painted in the early sixteenth century, and restored in 1970 and 1984. The Central Tower and South Transept roof (*right*). The South Transept roof was destroyed in the fire of 1984, but is now fully restored. The Chapter House roof (*below, left*), the oldest of the Minster's wooden roofs; and the great East Window (*below, right*), the largest expanse of stained glass in England.

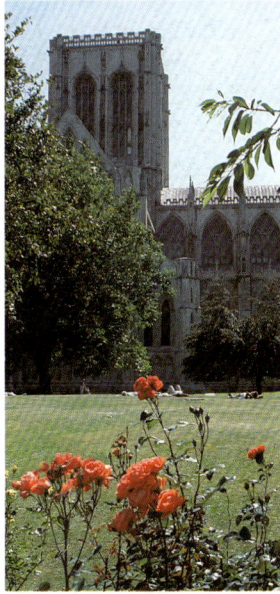

A Choir Screen roof boss (*far left*); the Minster from the north (*left*); the Nave from the east (*below*). The Five Sisters Window (*below, left*), is the largest thirteenth-century window in the world. It was re-leaded in the 1920s, using lead from Rievaulx Abbey, North Yorkshire, which was ruined during the Dissolution.

The doorways of York are one of the city's most attractive features, ranging from Norman through to medieval and Georgian. Pictured (*right*) is a Georgian doorway in Petergate.

Special
of
The Day
'CANDLELIT'
Dinner
SERVED FROM 6 PM

Dinner
and
Barfood
Served
from 6pm

Opposite page: St William's College (*top, left*); the Guildhall (*top, middle*); the Bar Convent (*top, right*); High Petergate (*middle*); and the Mansion House (*bottom*).

Micklegate (*right and below, right*) and the Minster Library (*below*).

King's Manor (*left*). Originally the home of the Abbot of St Mary's, it was given by Henry VIII as the home of the King's Council in the North. The Arms of Charles I are incorporated over the doorway. St William's College courtyard (*right*); and (*below*) an unusual view from Stonegate.

St William's College (*left*); the Jorvik Viking Centre (*right*); Stonegate (*below*); and St Mary's Abbey (*below, left*).

Of the original 40 medieval parish churches in York, some 20 remain, although not all are still in use. Those which have become redundant have been found exciting new uses — an Old Persons' Centre; home of the exhibition, 'The York Story'; archaeological research; a Christian centre; an arts centre — not forgetting a dwelling house. Together they form a great architectural feature of the city. Pictured (*right*) is Holy Trinity, Goodramgate.

St Mary's, Castlegate (*left*) once a redundant medieval church, now the home of the exhibition 'The York Story', and a heritage centre; and (*below*) All Saints, Pavement. In medieval times, a lantern placed in the octagonal tower of All Saints acted as a beacon for travellers in the Forest of Galtres, north of the city. The Central Methodist Chapel (*right*); All Saints, North Street (*far right*) which has the finest collection of parish church stained glass in the city; and Holy Trinity, Goodramgate (*below, right*), an oasis of tranquillity. The church is known to date from the twelfth century, and has an unspoiled eighteenth-century interior.

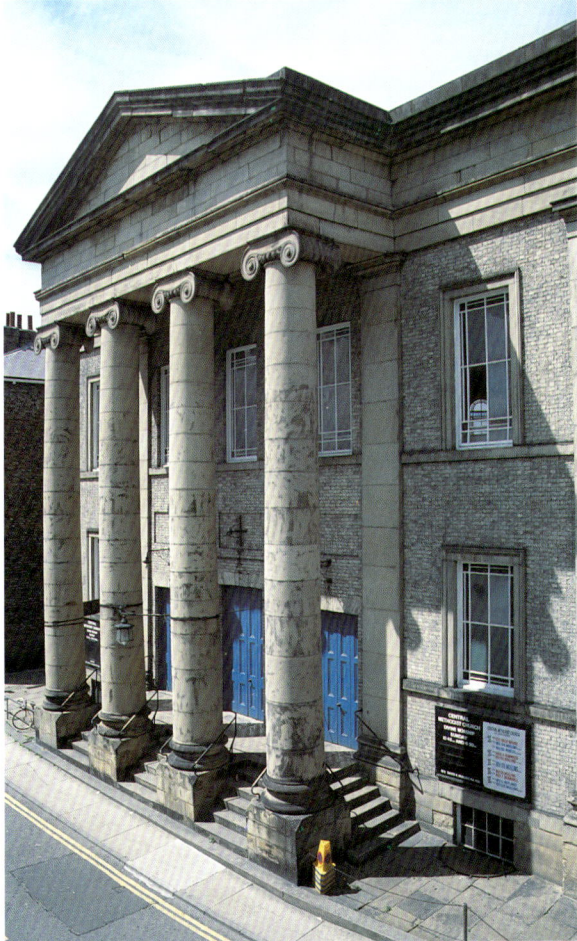

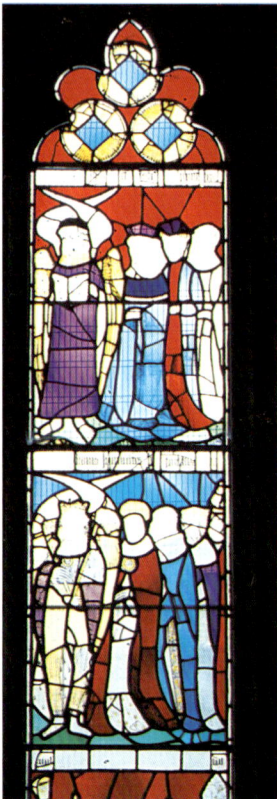

Opposite page: St Martin-le-Grand, Coney Street, was destroyed in the 1942 air raid. These gargoyles (*top and middle, left*) were saved and remain on the site, part of which has been restored. The remainder is a garden of remembrance. The clock at St Michael, Spurriergate (*top, right*) has one of the oldest movements in York. Holy Trinity, Goodramgate (*below, right*); and some of the magnificent stained glass in All Saints, North Street (*below, left*).

St Saviour's (*left*); St Sampson's (*right*); and (*below*) All Saints, North Street.

All Saints, North Street — a detail from the chancel roof (*above, left*) and stained glass (*left*); St Denys, Walmgate (*above*); and St Helen's Church, St Helen's Square (*far left*).

In York it is not only the great 'set pieces' which make it such a superb city; it is the hundreds of 'minor pleasures' which abound, many of them on the upper storeys of buildings, which call not only for looking but for seeing. Together, they make a leisurely stroll around the old streets a fascinating experience. So — look up and about you — and inside the buildings, too — for example, at this two-headed medieval roof boss in the Guildhall (*right*).

A firemark (*left*) on a wall denoted the insurance company with whom the building was insured. This one dates from the nineteenth century. Detail on a shop, Coney Street (*right*); the Beckett Arms (*below, left*); and an unusual tobacconist's sign (*below, right*).

William Etty (*above*) outside the Art Gallery; early cinema front, Fossgate (*top, middle*); tea shop sign, Stonegate (*top, right*). Guy Fawkes plaque in Stonegate (*below*), and St Martin's, Coney Street (*right*). The clock of St Martin's was first fitted on its bracket in 1668. It was a victim of the 1942 air raid which destroyed the church, but was restored in 1966. It is topped by 'the little admiral', the figure of an eighteenth-century naval officer using a sextant. The gilded head of Father Time is a replacement — the original one, badly charred, was sold for £1 in the 1960s.

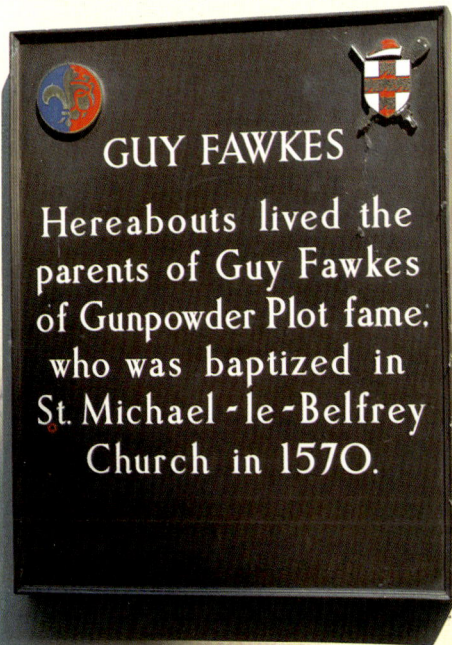

GUY FAWKES

Hereabouts lived the parents of Guy Fawkes of Gunpowder Plot fame, who was baptized in St. Michael-le-Belfrey Church in 1570.

A medieval boss in the Guildhall (*left*); a torch snuffer, Duncombe Place (*right*); and (*below*) the Golden Fleece pub sign.

Opposite page: The horned red devil (*top, left*), and ship's figurehead (*top, right*), both in Stonegate. Jane Wright monogram (*middle, left*); Doctor's sign, Stonegate (*middle, right*); a medieval carving, North Street (*bottom, left*); a detail on Lendal Bridge (*bottom, right*).

LITTLE STONEGATE

W
1675

J.H. GOSTLING
G.W. GOSTLING

The Red House, Duncombe Place (*left*); the plaque on the Roman column outside the Minster (*top, left*); Richard III plaque (*top, right*); Norman house plaque, Stonegate (*right*); a firemark, Bootham (*below*); the King's Square cat and pigeon (*below, right*); and cholera burial ground outside the city walls (*below, left*); and (*bottom*) York's shortest street.

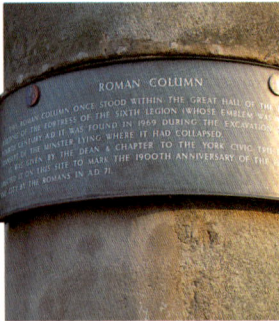

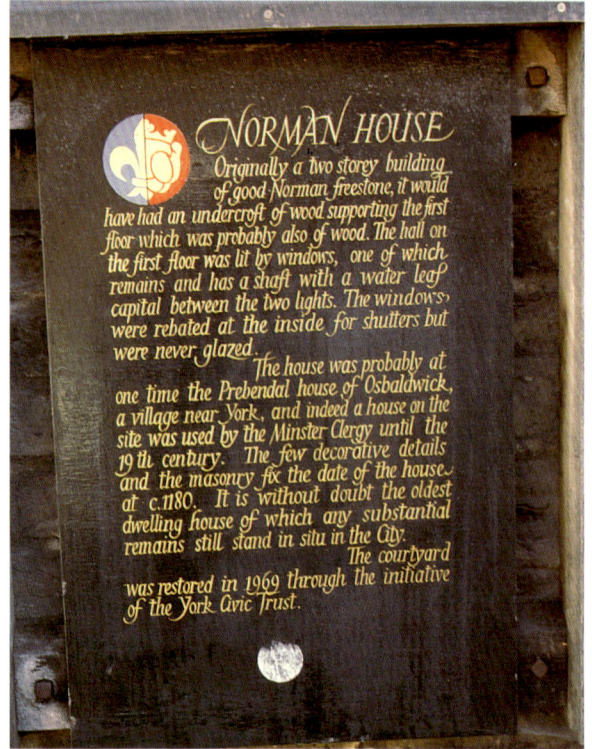

RICHARD III

Within the Archbishop's palace here.
King Richard III invested his son
as Prince of Wales
on the 8th September. 1483.

ROMAN COLUMN

NORMAN HOUSE

Originally a two storey building of good Norman freestone, it would have had an undercroft of wood supporting the first floor which was probably also of wood. The hall on the first floor was lit by windows, one of which remains and has a shaft with a water leaf capital between the two lights. The windows were rebated at the inside for shutters but were never glazed.

The house was probably at one time the Prebendal house of Osbaldwick, a village near York, and indeed a house on the site was used by the Minster Clergy until the 19th century. The few decorative details and the masonry fix the date of the house at c.1180. It is without doubt the oldest dwelling house of which any substantial remains still stand in situ in the City.

The courtyard was restored in 1969 through the initiative of the York Civic Trust.

CHOLERA BURIAL GROUND

Specially acquired for the burial of some of the 185 victims of a plague of cholera which lasted from 3rd June to 22nd October 1832. There are 20 surviving memorial stones, all of sandstone.

WHIP-MA-WHOP-MA-GATE

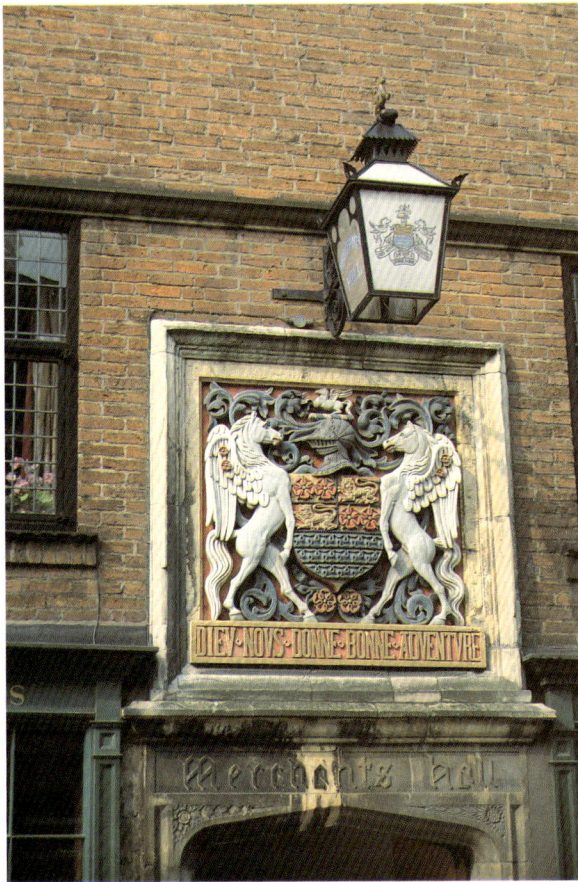

The Merchant Adventurers' Hall, Fossgate (*left*); St William's College entrance (*top, right*); the Norman house, Stonegate (*middle, right*); a detail on Lendal Bridge (*below, right*). Minerva — the Roman Goddess of wisdom and drama (*above*), with a pile of books, looks down from the corner of Minster Gates, at one time known as 'Bookbinders' Alley'. It is a continuation of Stonegate, which used to be where York's bookshops could be found. The stocks in the churchyard of Holy Trinity, Micklegate (*bottom*).

ACKNOWLEDGMENTS

The majority of photographs in this book were specially commissioned; others supplied to us or requiring acknowledgment are listed below.

p5 By courtesy of the Trustees of the British Museum. p7 By kind permission of the Dean and Chapter of York. p9 By kind permission of North Yorkshire County Library. p12 Reproduced by kind permission of the National Portrait Gallery, London. p13 By courtesy of Sotheby's, London. p14 By kind permission of the National Railway Museum, York. p15 (*top and bottom, right*) By courtesy of Rowntree Archives, Rowntree Limited, York. p15 (*bottom, left*) By courtesy of Terry's Group, York. p16 By kind permission of York City Archives. p17 By kind permission of York City Archives. p47 (*top, left*) and (*bottom*) By kind permission of the National Railway Museum, York. p55 (*top, middle*) By kind permission of the Jorvik Viking Centre.

Printed in England